CAST  IRON
COOKING FOR
VEGETARIANS

{ *Also by Joanna Pruess:* }

The Supermarket Epicure: *The Cookbook for Gourmet Food at Supermarket Prices*
D'Artagnan's Glorious Game Cookbook
Eat Tea/Tea Cuisine: *A New Approach to Flavoring Contemporary and Traditional Dishes*
Supermarket Confidential: *The Secrets of One-Stop Shopping for Delicious Meals*
Soup for Every Body: *Low Carb, High Protein, Vegetarian and More*
Fiamma: *The Essence of Contemporary Italian Cooking (with Michael White)*
Seduced by Bacon: *Recipes and Lore about America's Favorite Indulgence*
Mod Mex: *Cooking Vibrant Fiesta Flavors at Home (with Scott Linquist)*
Cast Iron Cookbook: *Delicious and Simple Comfort Food*

CAST IRON
COOKING FOR
VEGETARIANS

JOANNA PRUESS
PHOTOGRAPHY BY BATTMAN

Skyhorse Publishing

Skyhorse Publishing books may be purchased in bulk at special discounts for
sales promotion, corporate gifts, fund-raising, or educational purposes. Special
editions can also be created to specifications. For details, contact the Special Sales
Department, Skyhorse Publishing, 307 West 36th Street, 11th Floor, New York,
NY 10018 or info@skyhorsepublishing.com

www.skyhorsepublishing.com

Library of Congress Cataloging-in-Publication Data is available on file.

ISBN 978-1-62914-324-8

All photography by Battman, except for istockphoto images on pages 115, 189, and
190 and shutterstock on page 214.

Printed in China

To Nicole, Ben, and Justin: You are, as always, my source of pride and inspiration.

And for my late mother, Harriet Rubens, who worked very hard to remember those recipes from so long ago.

"One is considered fortunate nowadays if by chance one of these iron utensils is handed down to them from the second to the third generation."

—*Aunt Ellen*

CONTENTS

LUNCHEON & OTHER NIBBLES 1

VEGETABLES & OTHER SIDES 23

MAIN COURSES 45

DESSERTS 67

SAUCES & STOCKS 91

APPENDIX 102

Acknowledgments

My profound thanks go to:

First, Ann Treistman, my wonderful editor at Skyhorse Publishing, for another timely idea that evoked many happy memories, and for shepherding this project through with passion and wisdom;

Alan Batt (Battman) for your evocative photographs, easy disposition, and for going far beyond the call of duty to make the food look so real and tempting;

LeAnna Weller Smith, designer, for perfectly capturing the spirit of yesterday and today in this book and your generous, creative spirit;

David G. Smith—a.k.a. the Pan Man—for expert guidance in all matters relating to cast-iron cookware, including the history and care, and for loaning me archival materials;

Joel Schif—a prominent disciple of antique cast-iron cookware, and generous source of printed materials and information;

and to Jane Crosen for your copyediting and amusing, informative insights.

Thanks to the following for your pots and palates, testing and other useful thoughts:

Haejin Baek, Michael Berk, Sarah and Glenn Collins, Moira Crabtree, James Derek, Joe DiMaggio, Jr., Bobbie D'Angelo, Teresa Farney, Dianne Flamini, Lucio Galano and Louis Valantasis, Clara, Tony and the entire Grande family, Pam and John Harding, Elyse and John Harney, Bob Lape, Deb Lape Lackowski, Lisa Ligas, Stephen and Sally Kahan, Carole and Winston Kulok, Sally and Gene Kofke, Geri and Kit

Laybourne, Michael Pesce, Jane and Jack Quigley, Wendy Raymont, Janet Roth, Dick Saphir, Kathy and Tim Scheld, Anne Semmes, Roberta and Sandy Teller, Debbie Lewis, and Judi Arnold of Dufour Pastry.

Thanks to Rick Waln who has helped me in so many different ways.

Finally, to the relatives, acquaintances, and friends over the years who left us recipes and happy food memories. . . .

Introduction

L ife certainly seems more challenging today, even compared with just a few years ago. Whether those earlier times were ever really kinder and gentler, or just rose-colored dreams, is debatable. For whatever the reasons, these days many of us crave the comfort of the familiar in one form or another. That yearning is most obvious in our food choices: simplicity is the new sophistication and fussy fare seems dated.

Mac and cheese—just like Mom's or dressed up—appears on restaurant menus. Even in fancier restaurants, some homey dishes like Brussels sprouts are served in the same cast-iron ramekins and casseroles in which they are cooked, sometimes smugly sharing the table with Limoges porcelain.

Old-fashioned fare and cookware not only satisfy our hunger, on a primal level they reassure us by their link to the past . . . and seem so right for today.

Old Is Newsworthy

Long before my great-grandmother simmered chicken and dumplings in her Dutch oven, cast-iron cookware was appreciated. The Chinese began melting and forming the metal into vessels in the sixth century BCE. By the Middle Ages, tools and cookware that were cast in iron were so valuable they were listed as hereditary property in European estates; and in the fifteenth century, three-legged, dark gray iron cauldrons were common in hearths and fireplaces.

The pots arrived in the New World with the earliest European settlers. By the mid-nineteenth century, as Americans pushed beyond the Mississippi River across the plains to the Old West, thousands of pioneers hitched their oxen or mules to covered wagons. Often, a thick-walled pot with a tight-fitting lid—the Dutch oven—was on the back of each chuck wagon. It was essential for cooking meals.

For the forty-niners who went to California during the Gold Rush, "cooking was in black iron spiders (monumental cast iron frying pans on legs, originally designed for open hearth cooking and now pressed into service over the campfire) and Dutch ovens. Meals were dished up with the sky as roof and the earth as dining table, around a fire of sage, twigs, or buffalo chips," writes Ann Chandonnet in *Gold Rush Grub: From Turpentine Stew to Hoochinoo*, (University of Alaska Press, 2006).

David G. Smith, a pre-eminent cast-iron cookware historian (a.k.a. the Pan Man), veteran collector, and co-founder of the Wagner and Griswold Society (www.wag-society.org), says that the first piece of cast-iron cookware made in the American Colonies was a small kettle cast in 1642, in Lynn, Massachusetts.

Today, celebrated chefs and cooks like Emeril Lagasse, Tom Colicchio, and Martha Stewart are among many who have joined the cast-iron bandwagon as enthusiastic advocates.

Why Cast-Iron Now?

Teresa Farney, a friend and food editor of the Colorado Springs *Gazette*, asks: "Do you really need to dish out hundreds of dollars for designer-label, high-end cookware when there's good old cast-iron around? Durable, functional, and relatively inexpensive, cast-iron has so much going for it, it's a wonder more cooks don't use it. Maybe it's because cast-iron seems so old-fashioned compared to all the modern-looking $300-plus industrial cookware sets."

"Among its strengths is that the heavy metal retains heat well, which helps food cook quickly and evenly," Farney adds. The reason many people say that they buy a large black skillet in the first place is because they remember their mom or grandmother using it to make the best fried chicken and wonderfully crusty loaves of breads. As a result of that weight—the cookware's only major drawback—the pans take longer to heat up than, say, stainless steel or aluminum. A quick rule of thumb is to allow 3 to 4 ½ minutes, depending how hot the recipe says the pan should be. Since the handles are also made of metal, they also get hot, so a mitt is essential.

Cast-iron pots and pans are ideal for braising comfort-style dishes over low heat, as well as searing foods over high heat on top of the stove and then finishing them in the oven. Throughout this book, I use every cooking technique from searing and sweating foods to simmering and frying—both deep fat and pan-frying—as well as caramelizing. The cookware can also go directly from the stove to the table.

Another friend, Marguerite Thomas, who writes for the Los Angeles Times International Syndicate, adds that the pans are wonderful on an induction cooktop, unlike those made of either copper or aluminum, which do not conduct (or "induce") magnetic energy from the cooktop and thus can't cause metal vessels to heat up. The only place cast-iron doesn't work is in a microwave.

With regards to what can be cooked in cast-iron, I say just about everything. When I was just learning to cook with cast-iron, I remember being told not to use the pans for tomatoes or other acidic foods because the metal can discolor or turn them bitter. Over the years, however, and especially while testing the recipes in this book, my experience has been that if the pan is well seasoned, this isn't a problem. That said, when cooking a lot of tomatoes, where using cast-iron serves no real purpose in the recipe and/or the sauce is made separately anyway, I'd use a non-reactive skillet or pan, such as stainless steel. What I wouldn't do is store cooked foods for a long time in the pots.

Once cast-iron pans are seasoned (see pages xxiii to xxvi) and with minimal care—basically wiping and drying them over low heat, then spreading a thin layer of shortening or even non-stick vegetable spray over them—they improve with use, developing that shiny surface that makes them so good for nonstick cooking without added fat. Their biggest foe is being ignored.

The pans are also an investment in the future and the health of our planet: Long after many expensive pots and pans (especially those with nonstick surfaces which can deteriorate over high heat) have been discarded, your cast-iron cookware will be serviceable and can be passed down to future generations. Even those that have been seriously abused can be cleaned and re-seasoned, and there are tons of gray iron pots and pans in attics and at yard sales waiting to be adopted.

Incidentally, did you ever hear of anyone in your grandparents' generation with anemia? "Iron-poor blood" was pretty rare, since the tiny bit of iron that reacts with food supplies that essential nutrient to stave off the deficiency.

Craving Foods from Yesteryear

As for why we are craving comfort food now, John DeLucie, the chef at The Waverly Inn in New York, writes in his memoir, *The Hunger* (HarperCollins, 2009), "After 9-11, New Yorkers were hankering for a nostalgic take on American dishes from a more innocent time. Nothing too fancy or 'chefy' as the partners liked to say," referring to how he made his mac and cheese exceptional with truffles shaved on top.

"Real" foods—even if somewhat embellished—don't require mental gymnastics to appreciate. Their aromas and tastes can carry us back to more reassuring days shared with family and friends. Like the bite of tea-soaked madeleine that opened the floodgates to Marcel Proust's past, my re-creation of Tamale Pie—a favorite cornbread topped Tex-Mex casserole—instantly transports me back to my childhood in Los Angeles. Similarly, while I've removed the chicken or skirt steak from my Vegetarian Fajitas, those satisfying rolls remain satisfying memories of my youth.

From the earliest days, Americans have used cast-iron skillets to bake desserts like Raspberry-Blackberry Crisp and Ginger-Spice-Topped Peach Cobbler because they are simple and the results are so rewarding. The same is true of the German Apple Pancake or *pfannkuchen* I used to make to the delight of my kids. As for Apple-Cherry Tarte Tatin, the renowned French upside-down fruit tart recalls my years in Paris.

Connections to the Past and Future from around the World

Today the tradition of America as a melting pot continues as new flavors and dishes are introduced with each wave of immigrants. Because of these newcomers, the media, and advances in transportation and technology, we have more diverse ingredients available and we are more open to new preparations. Dishes that once were difficult to re-create are being made with ease across our country.

Yet, for many of us, time remains the biggest challenge to preparing good meals, and I appreciate ways to cut corners without compromising the quality of the food. In some recipes, I use conveniences items that didn't exist until fairly recently. For example, the all-butter puff pastry I buy for the Provençal Onion, Tomato, and Olive Tart and for Tarte Tatin helps me to make these dishes more easily and better; and high-quality purchased pizza dough and sauce put the "easy" in Easy Chicago-Style Pizza. Lest you think that most cast-iron dishes take a lot of time, I suggest you try Crustless Zucchini, Mushroom, and Cheddar Quiche for Two or the amazingly simple Chocolate Omelet Soufflé. It's not only quick to make, it's a decadently delicious dessert.

Through sharing recipes with old and new friends, I realize that we can derive comfort from unfamiliar dishes as well as those we already know, so long as they please our palates and don't seem like work to understand. When I perceive a link to how foods of different cultures are woven into our collective palate, they become more exciting to me.

These days, I enjoy exploring vegetarian dishes like Kale, Chickpeas, Yam, and Couscous Stuffed Bell Peppers. Even friends with hearty appetites find the dish extremely satisfying. These foods are homey and nurturing in tough times. I've also included Posole, a simple stew made with hominy, corn, and tofu, from the Native Americans of our Southwest.

Vegetable lovers (and even those who aren't) will find that cooking in cast iron coaxes flavors that are unachievable and more appealing than those resulting from any other cooking methods. Try Oven-Roasted Asparagus with Macadamia Nuts or Brussels Sprouts with Pistachios.

A Return to Home Cooking

Finally, if the economy has a bright side, it's that this austere climate has brought people back to their kitchens and dining tables. Today we are participating more in our food choices and once again entertaining friends and family at home, often in more relaxed settings. And "the more people cook, the healthier they are," says Michael Pollan, the award-winning author of *In Defense of Food* (Penguin Press, 2009).

I believe many of us want to recapture a sense of community and sharing that may have been lost over time. Cast-iron cooking is both a simple and rewarding way to start, as I hope you discover in this book.

—Joanna Pruess
New York, New York
November, 2013

Cleaning & Seasoning Cast-Iron Cookware

By David G. Smith, a.k.a. The Pan Man™

W ith proper care, your iron cookware will last forever and will require very little maintenance. If you have acquired a brand new pan, the manufacturer may have stated that it is "pre-seasoned." In most cases, this pre-seasoning is temporary. You will need to build up that seasoned surface. In this brief tutorial, I'll explain how to clean old pans, including rusted pans; how to season pans; and general cleaning and maintenance.

Initial Cleaning

CAUTION: Wear rubber gloves and eye protection while doing this!

Let's begin with an old piece of cast iron that is dirty, cruddy with burned-on food residue, and perhaps also slightly rusted. To initiate the cleaning process, begin by spraying the pan with oven cleaner, putting it in a plastic bag, and tying it shut. The bag will keep the oven cleaner from drying out, so it will continue to work. Leave the pan as it is for two or three days.

Then remove it from the bag, and scrub it with a brush—my favorite is a brass brush I found at the automotive counter of my local hardware store. This brush is marketed for cleaning white wall tires. It is just the right size for doing pans. You can also find brass brushes at the grocery store in the kitchenware aisle or even in your drugstore.

If all the burned on grease doesn't come off on this first try, repeat the process with the bag and the oven cleaner, concentrating the cleaner to the troublesome areas.

For cleaning many pieces at one time, you can prepare a soaking solution of one and a half gallons of water to one (18-ounce) can of lye in a plastic container. Lye, like oven cleaner, is very caustic and will burn you. Always wear rubber gloves.

Mix enough solution in the plastic container to cover the items to be cleaned. Leave the pieces in the soak for about five days; then scrub the pieces. You can use the lye mixture several times. (Be careful not to use oven cleaner or lye on aluminum, finished wooden handles, pans with porcelain or enameled finishes as they will be destroyed.)

Finish the cleaning process as above.

I DO NOT recommend the following methods of cleaning:

- **Open fire:** The intense heat can severely warp or even crack the piece.
- **Self-cleaning oven:** Although this doesn't hold as great a risk as throwing it in a fire, the intense heat of a self-cleaning oven can warp a skillet. There is also a risk of cracking the piece.
- **Sandblasting:** This is the cardinal sin for collectors. Sandblasting destroys the patina making the piece a dull gray color. Most collectors will not buy a piece that has been sandblasted.

To Remove Rust

Buff the pan with a fine wire wheel of an electric drill. Crusted rust can then be dissolved by soaking the piece in a solution of equal amounts of white vinegar and water for a few hours. Don't leave it longer than overnight without checking it. This solution will eventually eat the iron!

It is now important to neutralize and stop the action of the vinegar so it won't continue to attack the iron. To do this, apply the oven cleaner again and let the piece soak overnight. You can also soak the piece overnight in an alkaline solution, such as washing soda, which is available in the cleaning department of most supermarkets and some hardware stores. Scrub the piece in dish detergent and hot water before seasoning.

Seasoning

After removing the burned-on grease, you are ready to season the piece. Preheat the oven to 125°F. This removes any moisture in the oven which could condense on the cold skillet, leaving a very fine gold or rust color.

Heat the piece in the preheated oven for about 15 minutes or until hot. Carefully remove the hot pan and apply shortening all over it. I prefer solid Crisco, but you can also ghee. I don't recommend oil, but it can be used. Solid Crisco will flow right on. Of course, you have to use a hot pad or rag to hold them.

Return the pots to the oven right side up and raise the temperature to 225°F. Leave them in the oven for 30 minutes, then remove and wipe off any pooled shortening, leaving the piece still shining wet. The timing is important here because if you leave them in the oven too long, the shortening begins to thicken.

Return the pieces to the oven for another 30 minutes. Remove and let them cool down for 10 to 15 minutes or until they are very warm but not too hot to work with, then wipe them to a dull shine. If the shiny surface resists wiping, the pan is too cool. The initial seasoning should be accomplished at this point. However, typical of cast-iron cookware, the more you use it (and don't abuse it) the better it will be.

It is generally recommended that you cook fatty foods in the pan the first few times you use it as this adds to the seasoning process. This goes for new pre-seasoned pans as well.

Before adding any fat to the pan when you're cooking, heat the pan for 3 ½ to 4 minutes over medium to high, until hot but not smoking, unless otherwise indicated in the recipe.

Routine Care

CAUTION: DO NOT put cold water in a hot pan! Cold water will crack a hot pan!

DO NOT use detergent to clean a cast-iron pan after cooking with it. That will destroy the seasoning. Instead, put hot water in the pan and bring it to a boil. Let the pan soak for several minutes, then wipe it out with a paper towel. If something sticks, scrape it with a spoon to dislodge it. Do not use a Brillo or other abrasive metal pads to scour the pan as they cut into the seasoned surface.

Next, reheat the pan and apply a fine coating of shortening, oil, or even a non-stick spray, such as Pam. It should just wet the surface and shouldn't run. Wipe off enough of the heated oil to leave the pan with a dull shine. As you use the piece and continue with this maintenance seasoning process, your pan will develop a nice black patina and a stick-free surface.

If you follow these suggestions, you'll be able to pass on your favorite skillets to your children and grandchildren! I know they last—I've been collecting cast iron for more than thirty years and currently buy and sell at www.panman.com. In addition, I coauthored *The Book of Griswold & Wagner* and *The Book of Wagner & Griswold*.

"The secret of good cooking is largely a matter of developing and enhancing the natural food flavors which the Griswold Dutch Oven does so well, because it retains the steam and conserves the natural juices of all foods cooked."

—*Aunt Ellen*

About Aunt Ellen

Write "Aunt Ellen," at the Griswold Kitchen, any time you want advice about recipes, or want more recipes, or want to know more about "Waterless Cooking" or Griswold "Waterless Utensils." The Aunt Ellen service is always free. The Griswold Mfg. Company, Erie, Pa.

Aunt Ellen was "born" in the 1920s, when Miss M. Etta Moses began fielding letters received at the Griswold Manufacturing Company about the use and care of the brand's cookware utensils.

She soon began offering recipes and advice on cooking with cast-iron, under the pen name "Aunt Ellen." Griswold's commercial cookware lines were founded around that time, and after World War II included complete kitchenware packages, so there was a need for a woman's voice in their ranks.

Aunt Ellen became so well-known that stacks of mail came across her desk every day for her hints and advice. And continued to do so for twenty-five years.

Miss M. Etta Moses died in 1948, after more than fifty years as a Griswold employee.

Her recipes and advice, included throughout this book, are as helpful and as much fun to read as they were nearly a century ago.

CAST IRON
COOKING FOR
VEGETARIANS

LUNCHEON & OTHER NIBBLES

Mom's Mac and Cheese
Serves 8

When I was growing up, my mother made scrumptious macaroni and cheese with creamy sauce, sautéed onions, paprika, and loads of Tillamook or sharp Cheddar cheese. My siblings and I loved it, especially the crunchy-cheesy topping. Mom baked the casserole in the cast-iron Dutch oven she received as a wedding present. I prefer to use a 10-inch skillet.

When I added Parmesan cheese and panko bread crumbs to the topping, my kids and friends attacked that mac with a vengeance, thus it took on the name "macattacaroni." My favorite pasta for this is cellentani, a tubular cork-screw shape that has a ridged surface.

Preheat your oven to 350°F. Bring a large pot of salted water to a boil. Add the pasta and cook until al dente, about 10 minutes; drain and set aside.

Meanwhile, heat a 10-inch Dutch oven or skillet over medium-high heat until hot. Add the oil and onions and cook until they are golden, about 4 minutes.

Add the butter and, when melted, stir in the flour and cook until lightly colored, about 3 minutes, stirring constantly. Whisk in the milk and bring to a boil, stirring until smooth. Reduce the heat and simmer for 10 minutes or until the sauce thickens, stirring occasionally. Add 3 cups of the

INGREDIENTS

- ½ pound uncooked elbow macaroni, cellentani, or other tubular pasta
- 1 medium yellow onion, peeled and diced
- 1 Tablespoon vegetable oil
- 1 to 2 Tablespoons unsalted butter
- 3 Tablespoons unbleached all-purpose flour
- 3 ¼ cups whole milk
- 4 cups (1 pound) shredded sharp Cheddar cheese
- 1 teaspoon salt or to taste
- 1 teaspoon paprika
- Freshly ground black pepper
- ½ cup grated Parmigiano-Reggiano cheese
- ⅓ cup panko bread crumbs, found in the Asian food section of supermarkets

cheese and stir until it has melted. Stir in the macaroni and season with paprika, salt, and pepper to taste.

Combine the remaining cup of Cheddar, the Parmigiano-Reggiano, and panko crumbs in a bowl. Spoon the mixture over the macaroni and bake for 30 minutes or until the top is golden brown. If it is not browned enough, turn the broiler on and cook for 3 to 4 minutes longer, watching carefully that it doesn't burn. Remove the casserole and cool for 5 minutes before serving.

Note: Try the following mac and cheese additions: diced, canned, or chopped sun-dried tomatoes; a small white truffle thinly shaved and/ or white truffle oil.

Provençal Onion, Tomato, and Olive Tart (Pissaladière)
Serves 4 to 6

Pissaladières are popular pizza-like snacks in the south of France. Some of the most delicious are made with puff pastry. Although my version isn't classic, friends love the generous tangle of sautéed onions, sun-dried tomatoes, and olives baked with the flaky crust on top, like a Tarte Tatin (page 75), then flipped before serving. The thin layer of caramel accents the tangy onions. The tart is best eaten soon after baking.

INGREDIENTS

1 (14-ounce) package all-butter puff pastry, defrosted according to package directions

¾ pound yellow onions, peeled, cut in half lengthwise and thinly sliced crosswise

2 Tablespoons olive oil

2 Tablespoons white balsamic vinegar

½ Tablespoon herbes de Provence

½ teaspoon salt

Freshly ground black pepper

3 Tablespoons sugar

1 ½ Tablespoons water

⅔ cup (3 ounces) sun-dried tomatoes, blotted dry and thinly sliced

⅓ cup (2 ounces) pitted oil-cured black olives, chopped

Preheat your oven to 425°F. Unfold the pastry and, using a circular pattern, cut it into an 11-inch round; lay the dough on a cutting board, cover with a towel, and refrigerate for hour.

Meanwhile, heat a 10-inch cast-iron skillet over medium-high heat until hot but not smoking, 3 ½ to 4 minutes. In a large bowl, combine the onions and oil; add them to the skillet and sauté over medium-low heat until they are golden, about 15 minutes, stirring often. Pour in the vinegar, raise the heat to high, and boil until the vinegar evaporates, about 30 seconds, stirring often. Scrape the onions into a bowl, then stir in the herbes de Provence, salt, and a generous amount of pepper.

Wipe out the skillet and heat it over medium-high heat. Add the sugar and water and cook until the sugar melts and turns a rich amber brown, about 5 minutes, rotating the pan to coat it evenly. Remove the skillet from the heat and spoon the onions over the caramel; scatter the tomatoes and olives evenly over the onions and lay the puff pastry on top, tucking the edges into the pan. With a sharp knife, make four or five 1-inch cuts in the top.

Bake in the middle of the oven for 10 minutes; adjust the heat down to 350°F and continue baking until the crust is puffed and golden, about 20 minutes. Remove and let it stand for 5 minutes. Run a knife around the edges of the pan to loosen the pastry, then place a 10-inch plate directly on the pissaladière and flip it out. Replace any ingredients that remain in the pan. With a serrated knife, cut the pissaladière into wedges and serve.

My Favorite Deep-Dish Vegetarian Pizza

Serves 4 as a main course

This substantial deep-dish pizza of broccoli, sun-dried tomatoes, olives, and artichoke hearts is topped with mozzarella and a final shower of fresh basil leaves. To me, this is comfort food. The cheese sprinkled over most of the ingredients prevents the ingredients from burning or drying out. Be sure to let the pizza rest once it comes from the oven; this way, the pizza will easily slide out of the skillet, and you won't burn your mouth.

INGREDIENTS

1 pound pizza dough, defrosted in the refrigerator, if frozen (see the recipe notes on page 10)

2 Tablespoons olive oil

1 small yellow onion, peeled and thinly sliced crosswise

1 cup purchased Italian tomato pasta sauce

2 large cloves garlic, peeled and minced

2 cups small broccoli florets, cooked

½ cup (2 ounces) sun-dried tomatoes in oil, blotted on paper towels and thinly sliced

⅓ cup (2 ounces) pitted oil-cured olives, chopped

1 ½ teaspoons dried oregano, crushed

Pinch of red pepper flakes, crushed (optional)

2 cups (½ pound) shredded low-moisture mozzarella

1 (6.5-ounce) jar marinated and quartered artichoke hearts, drained and blotted on paper towels

2 Tablespoons grated Parmigiano-Reggiano

2 Tablespoons julienned fresh basil leaves

Remove the dough from the refrigerator about 1 hour before starting to prepare the pizza. Preheat your oven to 500°F and position the rack in the lower third of the oven.

Heat a 10-inch cast-iron skillet over medium-high heat until hot but not smoking, 3 ½ to 4 minutes. Add 1 Tablespoon of the oil and the onions and sauté until they are limp and golden brown, about 3 minutes;

remove with a slotted spoon to a bowl. Wipe out the skillet and brush the bottom and sides with oil.

Work the dough into a disc about 12 inches in diameter, pressing from the center outwards with your fingertips and gently stretching it. Lay it in the skillet and gently push it up the sides, taking care not to tear it. If the dough extends over the edges, trim it even with the pan. The sauce will help hold it up.

Ladle on the sauce, spreading it with a spatula to within ½ inch of the edges; add the garlic, onion, broccoli, sun-dried tomatoes, and olives followed by the oregano, pepper flakes, and finally the mozzarella. Bake for 15 minutes; then add the artichoke hearts, sprinkle on the cheese, adjust the heat down to 400°F, and cook until the cheese is bubbling and golden brown, 8 to 10 minutes.

Remove the pizza from the oven and let cool for at least 15 minutes. Then, using a wide metal spatula, slide the pizza onto a cutting board. Sprinkle on the basil and, if desired, brush the crust with the remaining oil, then slice and serve.

Swiss Cheese and Apple Frittata

Serves 4 to 5 as a first course or light main course

When I first started making frittatas, they were usually with sautéed vegetables like zucchini and onions. But after developing the recipes for an article about the flat Italian omelets, I discovered numerous foods took well to the basic technique. For example, apples and cheese are often served together. I combined them with toasted almonds and onions into a savory appetizer or light main course. You can also cut a frittata into squares to serve as an hors d'oeuvre for 12 to 15 guests. In that case, you can make it ahead of time and serve it at room temperature.

INGREDIENTS

5 large eggs

½ teaspoon water

1 teaspoon finely chopped tarragon leaves

½ teaspoon salt, or to taste

¼ teaspoon ground nutmeg

⅛ teaspoon white pepper

2 Tablespoons unsalted butter

1 teaspoon canola or vegetable oil

1 medium yellow onion, peeled and chopped

2 medium Granny Smith or other tart green apples, peeled, cored, and chopped fairly fine

⅓ cup slivered almonds, toasted in a 350°F oven or toaster oven until lightly browned

1 cup (4 ounces) shredded Gruyère or other Swiss cheese

Chopped flat-leaf parsley, to garnish

In a large bowl, beat the eggs and water together. Stir in the tarragon, salt, nutmeg, and white pepper. Preheat your oven to 350°F.

Heat a 10-inch cast-iron skillet over medium-high heat until hot but not smoking, 3 ½ to 4 minutes. Add 1 Tablespoon of the butter, the oil, and chopped onion, and sauté until the onions are golden, 3 to 4 minutes, stirring occasionally. Add the apples and cook until limp, 3 to 4 minutes. Scrape them into the egg mixture, then add the slivered almonds and mix well.

Melt the remaining 1 Tablespoon of butter over medium-high heat; pour in the egg mixture, shaking to distribute the ingredients evenly. Cook for 1 minute, then sprinkle on the cheese and adjust the heat to low. After 10 minutes, loosen the edges with a metal spatula, gradually working under the entire frittata. Shake the pan to be sure it is detached. Transfer the skillet to the oven and bake until the eggs are set, 4 to 5 minutes. Remove, cut into wedges, and serve with a little parsley on top.

Huevos Rancheros
Serves 4 to 6

The combination of Cheddar cheese, corn, onions, and pickled jalapeños makes Mexican farmer-style eggs a tasty and colorful brunch option. Roasted frying peppers, cut in half lengthwise and laid flat in the skillet to cover the bottom before the eggs are poured in, help you to easily loft out each portion. Serve with refried beans and garnish with avocado slices. Once baked, the dish can stay for at least a half an hour in a slow oven.

INGREDIENTS

2 Tablespoons canola or vegetable oil

1 yellow onion, peeled and diced

2 Tablespoons softened unsalted butter

4 slices firm white bread

4 ounces thinly sliced Swiss cheese, preferably Gruyère or other imported cheese

4 ounces mixed mushrooms, trimmed, wiped, and sliced

Preheat your oven to 400°F. Lay the peppers directly on a gas or electric burner preheated to the hottest setting and roast until the skins are completely charred on all sides, including the ends, turning with tongs. Peppers can also be roasted under a broiler. Transfer them to a paper bag, close the top and let them steam for about 10 minutes to help remove the skin. Using a paring knife or your fingers, scrape off the blackened skin. Cut them in half lengthwise and remove the stem, seeds, and membranes.

Heat a 10-inch cast-iron skillet over medium-high heat until hot but not smoking, 3 ½ to 4 minutes. Add the oil and onion and sauté until it is lightly browned, 3 to 4 minutes, stirring often. Using a slotted spoon, remove it to a large bowl. Add another Tablespoon of oil and lay the peppers in a single layer, skin-side down, covering as much of the bottom as possible.

In a large bowl, beat the eggs and milk until blended. Stir in the cheese, corn, cilantro, jalapeños, and salt and black pepper to taste. Scrape the mixture into the skillet and cook for 1 minute over medium-high heat. Adjust the heat down to medium-low and cook for 10 minutes more.

Transfer the skillet to the middle of the oven, turn the heat down to 325°F, and bake until a knife inserted into the center comes out almost clean, 22 to 25 minutes. Remove and let stand for a few minutes before cutting into wedges. Spoon on some salsa and serve with a sprig of cilantro, a few avocado slices, and some refried beans, if desired.

Note: There are many recipes for fresh and cooked tomato salsa, as well as some terrific prepared products. I often buy chunky tomato salsa and add a pinch of chipotle chile powder for a hint of smoky heat.

Croque Monsieur
Serves 2

In France, when the proverbial ham-and-cheese sandwich is grilled, it rises to new culinary heights and is called a Croque Monsieur. Some versions are dipped in egg before cooking, but I think my vegetarian version is so easy and offers almost instant gratification. I like to turn the sandwiches a couple of times to get those appealing cross-hatch grill marks on the bread.

INGREDIENTS

2 Tablespoons canola or vegetable oil

1 yellow onion, peeled and diced

2 tablespoons softened unsalted butter

4 slices firm white bread

4 ounces thinly sliced Swiss cheese, preferably Gruyère or other imported cheese

4 ounces mixed mushrooms, trimmed, wiped, and sliced

2 Tablespoons softened unsalted butter

4 slices firm white bread

4 ounces thinly sliced Swiss cheese

2 Tablespoons canola or vegetable oil

4 slices, (preferably Gruyère or other imported) cheese

4 ounces mixed mushrooms, trimmed, wiped, and sliced

1 yellow onion, peeled and diced

Dijon mustard

Heat a cast-iron skillet over medium heat. Add oil and onions and sauté until the onion is soft, 3 to 4 minutes. Add the mushrooms and cook until wilted, about 3 minutes.

Heat a cast-iron grill pan or griddle over medium heat until hot but not smoking. Butter one side of each piece of bread. Lay the slices on a cutting board with the buttered sides down. Divide the cheese evenly among the four slices (you may have to fold the slices in half to fit the bread). Place an even amount of onions and mushrooms on each slice, spread each with a generous teaspoon of Dijon mustard, and then put the remaining two cheese-covered slices on top.

Put the sandwiches in the grill pan and cook for 1 minute, pressing lightly with a spatula; then turn and cook the other side for

1 minute. Turn the sandwich back over, cook for 1 minute or until the toast is golden brown; turn again and cook until both sides are golden, rotating them about a quarter turn from where the original grill marks are to finish cooking and create those attractive crosshatch grill marks. Remove the sandwiches from the grill, cut them into halves, and serve.

Spanish Quesadillas

Makes 8 triangles; serves 4 as an hors d'oeuvre or 1-2 for lunch

Quesadillas are typically Spanish, Mexican, or Southwestern American–style snacks made with white or whole wheat flour tortillas and melted cheese. (In Spanish, the word quesadilla means "little cheesy thing.") Once you've made a couple of quesadilla variations, you'll figure out many other possibilities. For example, these tasty triangles are filled with Spanish ingredients—Manchego cheese and jalapeños—and topped with Spanish smoked paprika.

INGREDIENTS

3 jalapeños

1 cup (4 ounces) shredded Manchego cheese

2 (10-inch) flour tortillas

Olive oil

½ Tablespoon small capers, blotted dry

Pinch of sweet Pimentón de la Vera (see note)

Heat a cast-iron skillet over medium heat. Add the jalapeños and roast until the skins are blackened. Place roasted jalapeños into a plastic bag until cool enough to handle, then remove the skins and chop.

Sprinkle half of the cheese evenly over one tortilla and cover with the jalapeños. Sprinkle on the capers, then cover with the remaining cheese and second tortilla.

Heat a 10-inch cast-iron skillet over medium heat until hot but not smoking, 3 ½ to 4 minutes; brush with a little oil. Put the filled quesadilla in the pan, brush the top with a little oil, and put a small skillet or pan on top and cook until the edges of the tortilla are browned, 2 to 3 minutes. With a wide spatula, flip the tortilla, and cook the other side until lightly browned, about 2 minutes. Remove the quesadilla, sprinkle on the Pimentón de la Vera, and let it stand for 1 minute; then cut into eighths with a pizza cutter or sharp knife, and serve.

Note: Spanish smoked paprika is known as Pimentón de la Vera. There are two varieties: sweet (*dulce*) and hot (*picante*). It is made from dried peppers that are slowly smoked over an oak fire for several weeks to impart the characteristic smoky flavor to many authentic Spanish dishes.

Asian Quesadillas

Makes 8 triangles; serves 4 as an hors d'oeuvre or 1-2 for lunch

Here's another global approach to quesadillas: pan-fried tortillas filled with zesty Chinese-flavored tofu topped with Jack cheese. While cheese isn't typical in Asian foods, I like this fusion of flavors.

INGREDIENTS

Canola or vegetable oil

5 ounces extra firm tofu, drained, cut into ½-inch cubes, and blotted dry on paper towels

3 Tablespoons finely chopped cilantro leaves

3 Tablespoons finely chopped scallion + thinly sliced scallion greens, to garnish

3 canned water chestnuts, finely chopped

3 Tablespoons hoisin sauce

1 ½ teaspoons soy sauce

1 teaspoon minced fresh ginger root

1 teaspoon hot chili oil

1 cup (4 ounces) shredded Monterey Jack or other mild cheese

2 (10-inch) flour tortillas

Heat a 10-inch cast-iron skillet over medium-high heat until hot but not smoking, 3 ½ to 4 minutes, and brush with 2 teaspoons of oil. Add the tofu. Cook until all sides are browned, stirring occasionally, about 5 minutes; stir in the cilantro, scallion, water chestnuts, hoisin, soy sauce, ginger, and chili oil. Scrape the mixture into a bowl and wipe out the skillet.

Heat the skillet over medium heat until hot but not smoking, 3 ½ to 4 minutes; brush with a little oil. Lightly brush one side of the first tortilla with oil and place it oiled-side down in the skillet. Spoon the meat evenly on top of the tortilla; sprinkle on the cheese and top with the second tortilla, lightly brushing the top with oil. Place a small heavy skillet (or pan with a can of food in it) on the quesadilla and cook until nicely browned, 1 to 1 ½ minutes, checking that it doesn't burn.

Turn the quesadilla and cook the other side until the cheese is melted and the tortilla is lightly browned, about 1 to 2 minutes more. Remove, cut into eighths with a pizza cutter or sharp knife, and serve.

VEGETABLES & OTHER SIDES

Mini Cast-Iron Skillet Cornbread
Serves 2 to 4

This toothsome cornbread made in a 6-inch skillet feeds two or four friends, depending on how hungry they are. Coarsely ground cornmeal, chopped jalapeños, and corn kernels add flavor and texture. I serve it with softened butter bumped up with a touch of honey or maple syrup.

A well-seasoned cast-iron skillet is essential for the crisp edges and golden brown crust. To preserve the crunchy texture, turn the bread onto a plate while still hot and leave it bottom-side up or serve it directly from the pan. This recipe is easily doubled. You'll also find those small skillets have a lot of other uses. (See note.)

Preheat your oven to 450°F. Put a 6-inch cast-iron skillet in the oven for 15 minutes to heat. Meanwhile combine the cornmeal, flour, sugar, baking powder, and salt in a bowl. Stir in the corn and jalapeños. In a separate bowl, whisk together the buttermilk, 4 Tablespoons of the butter, and the egg; stir the wet mixture into the dry ingredients until just blended.

Remove the skillet from the oven, brush with the remaining Tablespoon of butter, and spoon in the batter, smoothing the top with a metal spatula. Bake until the top of the cornbread is golden and a toothpick inserted in the center comes out clean, 23 to 25 minutes. Remove, and

INGREDIENTS

¾ cup coarsely ground yellow cornmeal

¼ cup unbleached all-purpose flour

1 Tablespoon sugar

1 teaspoon baking powder

½ teaspoon salt

½ cup defrosted frozen or canned corn kernels, drained

2 Tablespoons chopped pickled jalapeño peppers

½ cup buttermilk

5 Tablespoons melted unsalted butter

1 large egg

let stand on a rack for a few minutes before inverting (or serve the cornbread out of the pan). Serve with softened butter.

Note: Mini cast-iron skillets make appealing individual serving containers. For example, the Chocolate Chunk-Pecan Cookie Sundaes with Salted Caramel Sauce (page 96) are a decadent way to finish your dinner. Or, as Elyse Harney suggests, they are the perfect answer to breakfast for the "me generation." Elyse puts a small skillet on each of her stove's six burners and lets everyone make his or her eggs to their own taste. Some like them up; others prefer them over easy or scrambled, she says.

Sweet and Tangy Glazed Carrots with Cranberries
Serves 4

When honey and vinegar plus a handful of dried cranberries are reduced to glaze young carrots, it becomes a memorable side dish to enjoy for holidays or anytime you want a special vegetable. I like thyme honey because it adds a slightly bitter taste to the complex flavors, but any variety works. These can be made ahead and reheated.

INGREDIENTS

1 ½ pounds young carrots, peeled or large carrots cut lengthwise into quarters and in half widthwise

1 Tablespoon canola or vegetable oil

1 teaspoon salt

½ cup good-quality vegetable stock

1 Tablespoon unsalted butter

¼ cup dried cranberries

2 Tablespoons thyme honey or other variety

2 Tablespoons sherry or white wine vinegar

1 Tablespoon finely chopped flat-leaf parsley

Combine the carrots, oil, and salt in a bowl. Heat a cast-iron skillet large enough to hold the carrots in a single layer over medium heat until just hot, about 3 ½ minutes. Scrape the carrots into the pan oil and cook for 2 minutes, stirring once or twice. Stir in the stock and butter, cover the skillet, reduce the heat to low, and cook for 15 minutes or until the carrots are almost tender when pierced with the tip of a knife.

Remove the lid and stir in the cranberries, honey, and vinegar. Bring to a boil and cook until the liquid reduces to glaze the carrots, about 5 minutes, shaking the pan occasionally. Stir in the parsley and serve.

Glazed Butternut Squash
Serves 4 to 6

Butternut squash, luxuriously glazed with brown sugar, maple syrup, and bourbon, is so delicious, you may find everyone asking for seconds. The touch of minced fresh rosemary adds an exciting counterpoint to the sweet flavors. A few months ago I went looking for butternut squash and discovered that it is now more often sold already peeled and cubed, a welcome convenience.

INGREDIENTS

1 ¼ pounds peeled butternut squash, cut into 1-inch chunks

1 Tablespoon canola or vegetable oil

Salt and freshly ground black pepper

2 Tablespoons unsalted butter

2 Tablespoons firmly packed dark brown sugar

2 Tablespoons light amber maple syrup

2 Tablespoons bourbon

2 teaspoons minced fresh rosemary leaves (optional)

Toss the squash with the oil, about 1 teaspoon of salt, and pepper to taste. Heat a 10-inch cast-iron skillet over medium-high heat until hot but not smoking, 3 ½ to 4 minutes. Add the squash and cook until lightly browned on all sides, about 5 minutes, turning often.

Add the butter, brown sugar, and maple syrup; bring to a boil, and cook until the sugar is melted, turning to coat the squash. Off the heat, carefully pour in the bourbon (it might flame) and cook until the flames subside. Cover and cook over medium heat until the squash is almost tender, about 10 minutes, then uncover and gently reduce the liquid until it glazes the squash, about 3 minutes more, turning often. Stir in the rosemary, if using, and serve.

Zucchini Pancakes
Serves 6

Many vegetables other than potatoes can be shredded and fried into tasty pancakes. I particularly like this combination of zucchini, scallions, dill, mint, feta, and pine nuts. It reminds me of a pancake-like hors d'oeuvre called mücver that I've eaten on several occasions in Turkey. Serve the pancakes with a dab of Red Pepper–Yogurt Sauce or simply, as Turks do, with plain yogurt on top, either as a side dish or a nibble before a meal.

In a colander, toss the zucchini with about ½ Tablespoon of salt and drain for 20 to 25 minutes. Meanwhile, prepare the Red Pepper–Yogurt Sauce, if using, and set aside.

Working in batches, squeeze the zucchini with your hands to remove as much moisture as possible, then transfer it to a kitchen towel or several layers of paper towels and squeeze again. In a bowl, combine the zucchini, eggs, scallions, dill, mint or parsley, about ½ teaspoon of salt, and a generous amount of pepper, and mix well. Stir in the flour, then add the feta, and stir to blend. Just before cooking, stir in the pine nuts.

Preheat your oven to 300°F. Line a baking sheet with paper towels and put it in the oven.

Heat a 12-inch cast-iron skillet or griddle over medium-high heat until hot. Add enough oil to coat the bottom of the pan. Drop the

INGREDIENTS

1 pound zucchini, trimmed and coarsely grated by hand or in a food processor

Coarse or kosher salt

2 large eggs, beaten

1 cup chopped scallions, including most of the green parts

⅓ cup chopped fresh dill or 1 ½ Tablespoons dried dillweed

⅓ cup chopped fresh mint or flat-leaf parsley

Freshly ground black pepper

½ cup unbleached all-purpose flour

½ cup crumbled feta cheese

½ cup pine nuts

Olive oil, for frying

Red Pepper–Yogurt Sauce (page 93)

zucchini mixture by generous soup-spoonfuls into the skillet (about 3 Tablespoons) and flatten with the back of a spatula into 3-inch discs, cooking only as many pancakes as will fit comfortably without crowding. Fry until golden brown, 2 ½ to 3 minutes, then turn and fry the other side for the same length of time. Transfer the pancakes to the baking sheet to keep warm while frying the remaining pancakes. Serve hot.

Brussels Sprouts in Olive Oil with Pistachios

Serves 4

Forget the old-fashioned notion that everyone hates Brussels sprouts. This version—or one similar to it—is served by many of today's best restaurants to great acclaim. The Brussels sprouts are blanched in salted water to keep them bright green, then finished with pistachios.

Bring a pot of salted water to a boil. Add the Brussels sprouts and cook until just tender, about 3 minutes. Drain, rinse under very cold water to stop the cooking, and blot dry on a clean towel.

Add the oil, thyme, Brussels sprouts, and pistachios to a large cast-iron skillet and cook until heated through, turning often. Season to taste with salt and pepper, and serve.

INGREDIENTS

1 pound Brussels sprouts, outer leaves removed, cored and quartered lengthwise

Kosher salt

1 ½ Tablespoons olive or vegetable oil

Leaves from 2 sprigs fresh thyme, chopped

¼ cup (2 ounces) shelled pistachios

Freshly ground black pepper

Oven-Roasted Asparagus with Macadamia Nuts
Serves 4

If you haven't tasted asparagus roasted in the oven in a cast-iron skillet, you're in for a treat. The beautiful green stalks gain a depth of flavor impossible to achieve by simply boiling or steaming. Topped with chopped macadamia nuts and a little lemon zest, they are irresistible.

INGREDIENTS

1 pound medium asparagus, woody ends snapped off

1 Tablespoon extra-virgin olive oil

Coarse sea or kosher salt and freshly ground black pepper

1 Tablespoon unsalted butter

2 Tablespoons chopped macadamia nuts

1 teaspoon grated lemon zest

Preheat your oven to 450°F. Heat a 10-inch cast-iron skillet over medium-high heat until hot but not smoking, 3 ½ to 4 minutes. Add the asparagus, oil, about ½ teaspoon salt, and black pepper to taste, and shake to coat evenly. Place the skillet in the oven and roast until the stalks are bright green and crisp-tender with little char spots, about 10 minutes (or longer if you prefer them softer), shaking the pan occasionally.

Meanwhile, melt the butter in a small skillet over medium heat. Add the macadamias and cook until lightly browned, 2 to 3 minutes, watching that they don't burn. Stir in the lemon zest and keep warm over low heat.

When the asparagus are cooked, pour on the macadamia nuts and butter, turning to coat the stalks evenly, and serve.

Cheesy Stone-Ground Grits
Serves 6

If you haven't tried slowly simmered grits, liberally laced with Cheddar cheese, you're in for a treat. Although instant and quick-cooking grits are easier to find, coarse-ground grits produce an incomparably toothy yet creamy texture and satisfying taste. Given a choice, white grits are preferable to yellow, because they are less starchy, but both are delicious. Like hominy, grits are a Native American corn product. The dried and processed corn kernels are coarsely ground on a stone mill. In the South, devotees enjoy them at every meal from breakfast straight through dinner and dessert. I've found cooking times for grits from different suppliers can vary from under an hour to 2 hours. Stir the pot frequently, especially the bottom, with a flexible scraper and wait until after you've added the cheese to add salt.

Combine 2 cups of stock and the milk in a 10-inch cast-iron Dutch oven and bring a boil. Add the grits, stirring continuously until blended and smooth. Turn the heat down to low and simmer according to the package directions until the grits are tender, about 1 hour (some brands can take up to 2 hours), stirring frequently with a flexible scraper to prevent the grits from sticking to the bottom of the pan.

INGREDIENTS

2+ cups vegetable stock

2 cups whole milk

1 cup coarse stone-ground grits, preferably white

1 Tablespoon unsalted butter

2 cups (8 ounces) shredded sharp white Cheddar cheese

Salt

Tabasco or other hot sauce (optional)

If the mixture gets thick and starts to dry out, stir in more liquid—water or stock by ¼-cupfuls—until smooth. Once the grits are done, stir in the butter and cheese and cook until melted. Season to taste with salt and Tabasco sauce, if desired, before serving.

Blazin' Baked Beans

Serves 12

If you're a fan of baked beans with a little heat, this simple version— emboldened with chipotle chiles in adobo sauce—will assuredly excite your taste buds.

INGREDIENTS

2 pounds pea or navy beans, rinsed and picked over

1 Tablespoon salt or to taste

2 Tablespoons vegetable oil

1 ½ cups chopped yellow onions

2 chipotle chiles in adobo sauce, finely chopped

⅓ cup Dijon mustard

⅓ cup firmly packed dark brown sugar

1 (18-ounce) jar high-quality smoky barbecue sauce

Boiling water

Put the beans in a large cast-iron Dutch oven with enough water to cover. Bring to a boil and cook for 3 minutes; turn off the heat, cover, and let them stand for 1 hour. Drain, cover again with water, add salt, and bring to a boil for 5 minutes, then reduce the heat to a simmer, cover, and cook for 30 minutes more. Remove from the heat, pour the beans and their liquid into a large bowl, and let them stand in the liquid until cooled.

Meanwhile, preheat your oven to 250°F.

Heat a Dutch oven over medium-high heat until hot. Add the oil and onions and sauté until golden brown, 3 to 4 minutes.

Drain the beans and combine them with the onions, chipotle chiles, mustard, brown sugar, and barbecue sauce. Add enough boiling water to just cover the beans, cover the pot, and bake for 4 hours. Remove the lid for the last 30 minutes of cooking time, or until the liquid is reduced and the beans are very tender. Taste to adjust the seasonings, adding salt if needed. Let them stand for 15 minutes before serving.

MAIN COURSES

Savory Mushroom, Spinach, and Feta Bread Pudding
Serves 6 to 8

This simple-to-make bread pudding makes a sophisticated centerpiece for brunch, lunch, or on a buffet. Serve it with a green salad, if desired.

INGREDIENTS

2 cups whole milk

5 large eggs

1 teaspoon salt

Freshly ground black pepper

8 cups day-old French or Italian bread, roughly torn into 1 ½-inch cubes

3 Tablespoons olive oil

1 large yellow onion, peeled and diced

10 ounces mixed wild mushrooms, such as cremini, shiitake, and oyster, trimmed and sliced

2 large cloves garlic, peeled and minced

1 (10-ounce) package frozen leaf spinach, defrosted and squeezed very dry

6 ounces feta cheese, crumbled

1 Tablespoon finely chopped fresh thyme leaves

Nonstick vegetable spray

¼ cup grated aged Asiago cheese

In a large bowl, beat together the milk, eggs, salt, and black pepper to taste. Stir in the bread cubes, turning to coat evenly, and let them stand until the liquid is absorbed, about 15 minutes.

Meanwhile, preheat the oven to 350°F.

Heat a 10-inch cast-iron skillet over medium-high heat until hot. Add the oil and onions and sauté until golden, about 5 minutes. Stir in the mushrooms, and continue cooking until the mushrooms are wilted, stirring or shaking the pan occasionally. Add the garlic, cook for 1 minute, and then stir in the spinach. Gently fold the mushroom mixture, feta cheese, and thyme into the bread cubes.

Wipe out the pan if necessary. Spray the pan with vegetable spray. Scrape the mixture back into the skillet and bake for 40 minutes.

Sprinkle on the Asiago cheese and continue baking until the top is puffed and golden brown, about 10 minutes. Remove from the oven and let stand for a few minutes before serving.

Moroccan Vegetable Stew with Chermoula

Serves 6 to 8

When I visited Morocco, I sampled many flavorful vegetarian dishes, such as this colorful stew. It is finished with chermoula, a piquant condiment made with herbs and spices that is used throughout North Africa. Serve over couscous and, for added zest, use a tiny amount harissa, a peppery hot Middle Eastern sauce. Typically this dish would be cooked in a tagine, a conical-shaped clay pot.

INGREDIENTS

For the stew:

¼ cup olive oil

1 medium yellow onion, peeled and grated (about ½ cup)

1 teaspoon minced garlic

1 (14-ounce) can diced tomatoes, undrained

1 teaspoon sweet paprika

½ teaspoon ground cumin

½ teaspoon ground ginger

Generous pinch saffron threads

2 cups water

2 cups (about 8 ounces) baby carrots, peeled

2 cups (about 8 ounces) peeled parsnips, cut into ½-inch slices

2 cups (about 8 ounces) peeled butternut squash, cut into ¾-inch cubes

2 cups (about 8 ounces) small turnips, peeled and cut into ½-inch cubes

6 small Yukon gold potatoes, scrubbed and cut in halves or quarters, depending on size

1 cup vegetable stock or 1 additional cup water

12 small boiling onions, peeled

1 medium zucchini, cut in half and then into 1-inch lengths

Salt and freshly ground black pepper

For the chermoula:

¾ cup packed cilantro leaves

¼ cup packed flat-leaf parsley leaves

1 Tablespoon chopped garlic

1 Tablespoon sweet or smoked paprika

1 ½ teaspoons grated fresh gingerroot

2 teaspoons ground cumin

1 teaspoon ground turmeric

1 teaspoon ground coriander

⅛ teaspoon cayenne pepper

1 ½ tablespoons olive oil

1 Tablespoon freshly squeezed lemon juice

½ teaspoon kosher salt

4 to 6 cups cooked couscous, to serve with the stew

Heat a large cast-iron Dutch oven over medium heat until hot. Add the oil, grated onion, and garlic, and sauté until softened but not brown, about 2 minutes. Stir in the tomatoes, paprika, cumin, ginger, and saffron and bring to a gentle boil.

Add the water and carrots and cook until half-way done, about 10 minutes. Add the parsnips, butternut squash, turnips, potatoes, and stock. Lay a circular piece of parchment paper over the vegetables, cover the pan, and boil gently for 10 minutes.

Add the onions and zucchini, recover, and continue cooking until the vegetables are just tender when pierced with the tip of a knife. Season to taste with salt and pepper.

Meanwhile, prepare the chermoula: In a food processor, combine the cilantro, parsley, garlic, paprika, ginger, cumin, turmeric, coriander, and cayenne and pulse until roughly chopped. Add the olive oil, lemon juice, and salt and pulse into a chunky-smooth sauce. Adjust the seasonings to taste. Stir into the stew, and simmer briefly before serving.

Easy Shepherd's Pie
Serves 8

Lovers of this classic comfort dish who prefer not to eat meat can get plenty of protein by substituting lentils. This super easy dish, made with frozen cut-up vegetables, will appeal to all ages.

INGREDIENTS

2 pounds russet potatoes, peeled and cut into 1-inch cubes

⅓ cup whole milk

3 Tablespoons unsalted butter

Freshly ground black pepper

1 cup dry brown lentils, rinsed and sorted

1 bay leaf

2 cups water

3 Tablespoons olive oil

1 yellow onion, peeled and finely diced

4 ounces white mushrooms, wiped and sliced

1 teaspoon minced garlic

3 cups mixed frozen carrots, corn, green beans, and peas, defrosted

1 (14-ounce) can diced tomatoes, drained

¼ cup chopped flat-leaf parsley

1 Tablespoon Worcestershire sauce

1 teaspoon dried oregano

Salt and freshly ground black pepper

Tabasco Sauce (optional)

¼ cup grated imported Parmesan cheese

Preheat your oven to 375°F.

In a large pot, combine the potatoes with enough water to cover. Add salt and bring to a boil. Cook until tender when pierced with the tip of a knife, about 15 minutes. Drain, return to the pan, add the milk and butter, and mash with a potato masher until smooth. Season to taste with salt and pepper, cover, and keep warm.

Meanwhile, in a small saucepan, combine the lentils and bay leaf with 2 cups of water and bring to a boil; reduce the heat and simmer until the lentils are just about tender, 15 to 20 minutes. Take care not to overcook. Drain and set aside. Remove the bay leaf.

Heat a 10- or 11-inch cast-iron skillet over medium heat until hot. Add the oil and onions and sauté until lightly colored, 5 to 6 minutes. Add the mushrooms and cook until wilted, about 3 minutes, stirring frequently. Stir in the garlic and cook for 30 seconds longer.

Return the lentils to the skillet along with the defrosted vegetables, tomatoes, parsley, Worcestershire sauce, and oregano, and mix together. Bring the mixture to a boil over high heat; adjust the heat down to a simmer and cook the vegetables until tender, about 5 minutes, stirring often. Season to taste with salt, pepper, and Tabasco Sauce, if using.

Spoon the potatoes on top of the lentil-vegetable mixture and, using the tines of a fork, make a decorative pattern in them. Drizzle on the Parmesan cheese and run the casserole briefly under the broiler until the top is lightly browned, about 5 minutes, watching that it doesn't burn. Remove, let stand for at least 10 minutes, and serve.

Mexican Mac and Cheese
Serves 6

Classic mac and cheese takes a south-of-the-border turn with the addition of a chipotle in adobo, which imparts a hint of heat, and the crushed tortillas and Cotija cheese used for the topping. It's based on a recipe from chef Ivy Stark, with whom I coauthored the two Dos Caminos cookbooks. Serve with small bowls of sliced scallions, sour cream, sliced black olives, and pickled jalapeños, if you like.

INGREDIENTS

Salt

8 ounces uncooked wagon wheel macaroni

2 Tablespoons unsalted butter

¾ cup finely chopped onion

½ tablespoon minced garlic

1 teaspoon ground cumin

½ teaspoon ground coriander

2 Tablespoons all-purpose flour

2 cups milk

1 chipotle en adobo, minced

½ cup sundried tomatoes, thinly sliced

2 ¼ cups grated sharp Cheddar cheese

1 cup grated Jack cheese

1 ½ cups crushed tortilla chips

1 ⅓ cups freshly grated Cotija cheese

Bring a large pot of salted water to a boil. Add the pasta and cook according to package directions until al dente. Remove, drain, and set aside.

Meanwhile, heat a 10-inch cast-iron skillet over medium heat until hot. Add the butter, onion, garlic, cumin, and coriander, and cook over medium-low heat, stirring often, until the onion is softened, about 7 minutes.

Preheat your oven to 350°F.

Add the flour to the onions and stir continuously for 3 minutes. Whisk in the milk and bring to a boil. Reduce the heat and simmer for 2 minutes. Add the chipotle and tomatoes and cool slightly; add the cheeses and stir until melted. Stir the pasta into the cheese mixture.

In a bowl, toss the tortilla chips and Cotija cheese together and drizzle on top of the macaroni. Bake until the dish is hot and the top is golden brown, 25 to 30 minutes. Remove and let stand for 10 minutes before serving.

Crustless Zucchini, Mushroom, and Gruyère Cheese Quiche for Two

Serves 2

Quiche is a perennial favorite for a hearty breakfast, lunch, or light dinner. This crustless version for two is baked in a 6-inch cast-iron skillet and served straight from the oven. You can substitute any number of savory ingredients, including spinach or broccoli, as well as other kinds of cheeses.

INGREDIENTS

3 large eggs

¼ cup light cream or milk

½ teaspoon Dijon mustard

1 Tablespoon finely chopped fresh basil or flat-leaf parsley

Non-stick vegetable spray

1 ½ Tablespoons olive oil

½ cup (about 2 ounces) thinly sliced zucchini

½ cup thinly sliced yellow onion

¼ pound white mushrooms, wiped, trimmed, and thinly sliced

Salt and freshly ground black pepper

½ cup shredded Gruyère or Swiss cheese

In a bowl, beat together the eggs, cream, mustard, basil or parsley, and salt and pepper to taste.

Preheat the oven to 350°F. Lightly coat a 6-inch cast-iron skillet with non-stick vegetable spray.

Heat the skillet over medium-high heat until hot. Add the oil and zucchini slices in batches, and sauté until lightly browned on both sides, turning once. Using a slotted spoon, transfer the slices to the bowl with the eggs.

Add the onion to the skillet and sauté until golden; combine with the zucchini. Add a little more oil if needed, stir in the mushrooms, and sauté until wilted. Scrape into the bowl with the vegetables, and season with about a ½ teaspoon of salt, or to taste, and pepper. Stir in the cheese.

If needed, wipe out the pan. Spray again with non-stick spray. Scrape the egg mixture into the skillet and transfer to the oven. Bake until a knife inserted in the center comes out clean, about 30 minutes. Remove and serve with a spatula.

Kale, Chickpeas, Yam, Feta, and Couscous Stuffed Peppers
Serves 6

These colorful filled bell pepper halves are bursting with flavor and nutrition. Every meat-eater who has ever tried them has said they were completely satisfying. If you prefer, use quinoa rather than couscous. You can fill the peppers ahead and then bake them just before serving. They also reheat well in a microwave-safe dish. I use a red, orange, and yellow pepper.

INGREDIENTS	
2 Tablespoons extra-virgin olive oil, plus extra oil to brush on the peppers and pan	1 cup peeled and finely diced yams (about 5 ounces)
¾ cup finely chopped yellow onion	½ cup dried couscous
3 ounces white mushrooms, wiped, trimmed, and sliced	1 ½ cups vegetable stock
¼ cup finely chopped celery	½ cup drained petite diced tomatoes
1 ½ teaspoons minced garlic	½ cup chopped cilantro
½ tablespoon ground cumin	6 ounces crumbled feta cheese (about 1 ½ cups)
5 ounces kale, rinsed with a little water left on the leaves, stems removed, and chopped (about 6 cups)	Salt and freshly ground black pepper
	3 large bell peppers, cut in half lengthwise, seeds and membranes removed
1 cup canned chickpeas, rinsed and drained	Cucumber-Yogurt-Mint Sauce (page 95)

Preheat your oven to 350°F.

Heat a 10-inch cast-iron skillet over medium heat. Add the oil, onion, and celery and sauté until soft, 4 to 5 minutes, stirring often. Add garlic and cumin, and sauté for 30 seconds more. Add the mushrooms and sauté until softened; stir in the kale and cook until softened. Stir in the chickpeas, yams, couscous or quinoa, and stock; cover and bring to a boil. Reduce the heat and simmer until the quinoa is tender, about 5 minutes. Scrape into a large bowl, stir in the tomatoes, cilantro, 1 cup of the cheese, and salt and pepper to taste.

Wipe out the skillet. Brush the outsides of the peppers and the pan with a little oil. Lay the pepper halves in the skillet, cut side up, and spoon about 1 cup of filling into each, mounding it slightly in the center. Cover the pan tightly with aluminum foil and bake for 45 minutes. Uncover, sprinkle on the remaining cheese, and return to the oven until the tops are browned, about 15 minutes more.

Meanwhile, prepare the Cucumber-Yogurt-Mint Sauce (page 95). Remove the skillet from the oven, and let it stand for 5 minutes before transferring the peppers to plates and serving.

Vegetarian Fajitas
Serves 4

My family loves fajitas. They're versatile, easy to make, and appeal to all ages. This robust version includes bell peppers, onions, yellow and green squash, corn, and black beans seasoned with chili powder and minced pickled jalapeños. The filling is sprinkled with Jack cheese before being rolled in tortillas. Fajitas can easily be reheated in a partially covered microwave-safe dish.

Preheat your oven to 350°F. Wrap the tortillas in aluminum foil and heat in the oven until hot, about 15 minutes. Alternatively, once the filling is prepared, lay the tortillas directly on a flame on top of the stove, for a few seconds on each side, until little brown spots appear, turning once.

Heat a 10-inch cast-iron skillet over medium-high heat. Add the oil and onions, and sauté until the onions are soft and lightly colored, about 5 minutes. Add the pepper, zucchini, and yellow squash, and continue cooking until the vegetables are tender and lightly browned, about 15 minutes, stirring often.

INGREDIENTS

8 (8-inch) flour tortillas

2 Tablespoons olive oil

1 large yellow onion, peeled and cut crosswise into ¼-inch slices

1 large red bell pepper, seeds and membranes removed, cut into ¼-inch strips

2 cups julienned zucchini (about 8 ounces)

2 cups julienned yellow squash (about 8 ounces)

1 Tablespoon minced garlic

1 Tablespoon chili powder

¾ cup canned or defrosted frozen corn kernels

½ cup canned black beans, rinsed and drained

2 large scallions, trimmed and thinly sliced

1 Tablespoon minced pickled jalapeños (optional)

Salt and freshly ground black pepper

12 ounces shredded Jack cheese

1 ½ cups purchased tomato salsa

Add the garlic and chili powder and cook for 30 seconds; stir in the corn, black beans, scallions, and pickled jalapeños, if using. Season to taste with salt and pepper. Keep warm.

For each warm tortilla, spoon about ½ cup of the vegetables down the center, sprinkle on the cheese, roll up, and serve with a tablespoon or two of salsa drizzled on top.

DESSERTS

Raspberry-Blackberry Crisp
Serves 4 to 6

I don't like blueberries, which, I know, for many summer fruit lovers is a sin. On the other hand, I adore raspberries and blackberries, so when I make the proverbial summer fruit crisp—that generations of bakers have made in cast-iron skillets—they are the berries I choose. I think you'll find the combination is fabulous!

Preheat your oven to 375°F. Put a baking sheet in the middle of the oven. Lightly butter a 10-inch cast-iron skillet.

In a large bowl, stir the cornstarch and lemon juice together until blended; add the berries and sugar, and gently stir to combine them evenly. Scrape the mixture into the skillet.

In the same bowl, combine the oatmeal, flour, brown sugar, salt, and butter. Using a fork or your fingers, stir the mixture until it is crumbly and blended, and scatter it over the berries. Transfer the skillet to the baking sheet in the oven and bake until the topping is set and the berries are bubbling, about 40 minutes. Remove and cool for at least 15 minutes before serving the crisp from the skillet with vanilla ice cream or whipped cream on top.

INGREDIENTS

Unsalted butter to grease the skillet

1 Tablespoon + 1 teaspoon cornstarch

1 Tablespoon freshly squeezed lemon juice

4 cups mixed fresh blackberries and raspberries

½ to ⅔ cup sugar, depending on how sweet the berries are

⅔ cup quick-cooking oatmeal

⅓ cup unbleached all-purpose flour

⅓ cup firmly packed dark brown sugar

⅛ teaspoon salt

4 Tablespoons unsalted butter, at room temperature

Vanilla ice cream or sweetened whipped cream

Plum Clafoutis
Serves 6

Clafoutis is a classic French dessert—a puffy, custardy, fruit-filled pancake. Most often they are made with cherries, but my favorite fruit for this dish is plums. Serve it warm, straight from the pan either for brunch or dessert. Pfannkuchen (page 79) is another puffy pancake made with apples.

INGREDIENTS

½ cup unbleached all-purpose flour

½ cup + 3 Tablespoons sugar

Pinch of salt

1 cup whole milk

3 large eggs

1 teaspoon almond extract

2 Tablespoons unsalted butter

3 firm, ripe black plums (about 12 ounces), pitted and cut into medium slices

1 Tablespoon plum brandy or cognac Confectioners' sugar

Sweetened whipped cream or crème fraîche, to garnish

Preheat your oven to 425°F. In a large bowl, sift the flour, the ½ cup of sugar, and salt. In a small bowl, blend the milk, eggs, and almond extract together, and then whisk them into the dry ingredients until smooth.

Heat the butter in a 10-inch cast-iron skillet over medium heat until melted and bubbling. Stir in the plums and cook them for 2 minutes, or until almost soft, turning occasionally. Sprinkle on the remaining 3 Tablespoons of sugar, cook until the sugar is melted, then pour in the brandy or cognac and bring to a boil, shaking the pan to spread the fruit evenly.

Turn off the heat, pour the batter over the plums, and transfer the skillet to the oven. Bake until the clafouti is puffy, the edges are richly browned, and a knife inserted in the center comes out clean, about 18 minutes. Remove and let the clafoutis stand for 10 minutes, then sprinkle on some confectioners' sugar, and serve with a dollop of whipped cream or crème fraîche.

Ginger-Spice-Topped Peach Cobbler
Serves 8

Cobblers are among the most popular of Southern desserts. In this simple yet personal version, a ginger-spice batter is poured into the pan and topped by delicately rum-scented peaches. As it bakes, the crust rises to the top and almost covers the fruit. Serve the dessert directly from the skillet with ice cream or whipped cream.

Preheat your oven to 350°F. Put a baking sheet in the middle of the oven.

In a large bowl, stir the rum and cornstarch until smooth.

Add the peaches, sugar, and lemon juice and stir. Set aside.

In a 10-inch cast-iron skillet, heat the butter over medium heat until melted. Meanwhile, in a medium bowl, mix the flour, white and brown sugars, ginger, cinnamon, salt, and cloves. Whisk the milk and melted butter into the dry ingredients, leaving a thin coating of the butter on the bottom of the skillet.

Reheat the skillet over medium heat; pour in the batter and then add the peaches. Put the skillet

INGREDIENTS

Filling:

3 Tablespoons dark rum

2 ½ Tablespoons cornstarch

2 (16-ounce) packages frozen peaches, defrosted

1 cup sugar

2 Tablespoons freshly squeezed lemon juice

Topping:

6 Tablespoons unsalted butter

1 cup self-rising flour

⅓ cup sugar

⅓ cup firmly packed light brown sugar

1 Teaspoon ground ginger

½ teaspoon cinnamon

¼ teaspoon salt

⅛ teaspoon ground clove

1 cup whole milk

Vanilla ice cream or sweetened whipped cream, to garnish

on the baking sheet and bake until the cobbler's top is golden brown and the filling is bubbling, about 45 minutes. Remove from the oven and cool for at least 15 minutes, then serve the cobbler with vanilla ice cream or whipped cream.

Apple-Cherry Tarte Tatin
Serves 8

This famous upside-down tart of caramelized apples and puff pastry was first made by the two Tatin sisters from France's Loire Valley. There are countless versions, including this one in which the thick apple slices are complemented by tangy dried cherries. When I can find Jonagold apples, I use them because they are sweet and juicy with just a touch of tartness. They also hold together while baking.

In a small bowl, combine the cherries with the brandy and set aside. Roll out the puff pastry on a lightly floured surface to a thickness of ⅛ inch. With a sharp knife, cut it into an 11-inch circle and brush off any excess flour. Lay the pastry on a cutting board, cover with a towel, and refrigerate.

Peel and core the apples; slice them in half lengthwise, then cut each half in thirds lengthwise. Put them in a large bowl and drizzle with lemon juice as you cut them to prevent discoloring.

Preheat your oven to 400°F. Put the sugar in a 10-inch cast-iron skillet and drizzle on the water. Turn the heat

INGREDIENTS

¼ cup dried cherries

2 Tablespoons apple brandy or Calvados

1 (15-ounce) package all-butter puff pastry, defrosted according to package directions

5 to 6 medium firm, tart-sweet apples, such as Jonagold, Cortland, Northern Spy, Golden Delicious

Juice of 1 to 2 lemons

¾ cup sugar

1 Tablespoon water

4 Tablespoons unsalted butter, cut into small pieces

Crème fraîche or sweetened whipped cream, to garnish

to high and cook until the sugar melts into a rich, golden amber-colored syrup, 6 to 7 minutes, swirling and shaking the pan often to melt it evenly. Watch that it doesn't burn. Immediately remove the pan from the heat, add the butter (it might bubble up), and stir until it is incorporated. Continue stirring the mixture until the caramel cools, 3 to 4 minutes. If the sugar seizes up when you add the butter, return the pan to the heat to re-melt it.

Lay the apple slices on the caramel around the outside of the pan, on their side and each in the same direction with the stem end closest to the pan's edge. Put the remaining apple slices in the center. (You may not need all of the apples.) Drain the cherries and add them around the edges, between each apple slice, and in the middle.

Remove the puff pastry from the refrigerator and lay it over the apples, pushing the edges down the sides of the pan. Cut 3 or 4 small gashes in the surface of the pastry as air vents, then transfer the skillet to the oven and bake for 10 minutes. Reduce the heat to 375°F and bake for 20 minutes longer, or until the crust is golden brown and the syrup is bubbling up the sides.

Remove and cool the tart for about 20 minutes in the pan. Using a plate with a lip that is slightly larger than the skillet, put it upside down over the skillet and, holding them together with one hand, invert the skillet and let the tart slide out onto the plate, rearranging any apples that may have moved. Using a pie server with a sharp edge, cut the tart into slices and serve with a generous dollop of crème fraîche or whipped cream. You can also leave the tart in the pan and reheat it for 15 minutes in a preheated 375°F oven.

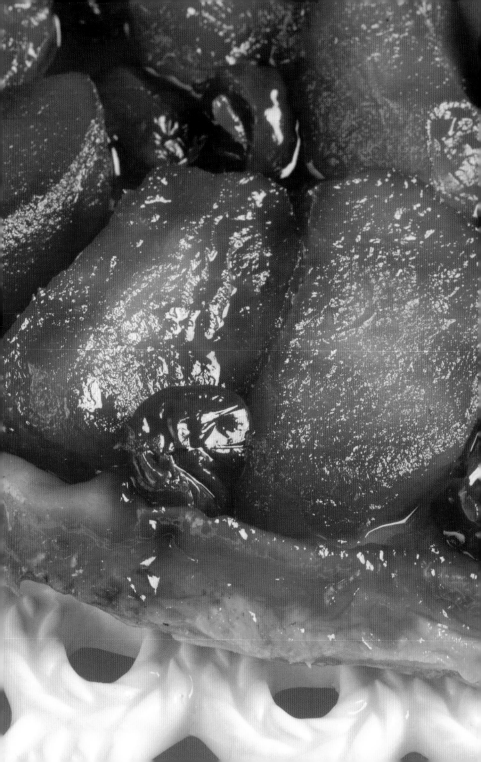

German-Style Apple Pancake (Pfannkuchen)

Serves 4

I remember making this German-style apple pancake for my kids as they were growing up. They were always wide-eyed with excitement as I took the puffy pancake from the oven and added the confectioners' sugar and lemon juice that were the final garnishes before we cut it up and devoured it. Don't worry if the pancake collapses. It'll still be delectable.

Preheat your oven to 400°F. Position the rack in the middle of the oven. Heat a 10-inch cast-iron skillet over medium heat until hot, about 3 minutes.

In a bowl, combine the apple slices with 1 Tablespoon of the lemon juice and set aside. In a large bowl, beat together the egg yolks, milk, sugar, cornstarch, salt, and lemon zest. In a separate large bowl, whisk the egg whites into soft peaks. Using a flexible spatula, gently fold the yolks into the whites until just mixed.

Add the butter to the heated skillet. When the butter foams, add the apples, turning to coat them with butter, and then arrange them in a single layer. Pour the egg mixture evenly over the apples. Partially cover, and cook for 10 minutes. Uncover the skillet, transfer it to the oven, and bake for about 15 minutes, or until the bottom of the *pfannkuchen* is nicely browned and it is set in the middle.

Remove, sprinkle with the confectioners' sugar and remaining lemon juice, and serve immediately.

> INGREDIENTS
>
> 1 large tart-sweet apple, such as Cortland, peeled, cored, and thinly sliced
>
> Juice and grated zest of 1 large lemon
>
> 4 large eggs, separated
>
> ½ cup whole milk
>
> 2 Tablespoons sugar
>
> 2 Tablespoons cornstarch
>
> ½ teaspoon salt
>
> 2 Tablespoons unsalted butter
>
> Confectioners' sugar, to garnish

Tuscan Pineapple Upside-Down Cake
Serves 8

Some years ago while visiting my friend, food writer Nancy Harmon Jenkins, in Tuscany, we had lunch with her neighbor, Mita Antolini, a local farmer. Mita made her "special dessert" in an old wood-burning stove. To my surprise, it turned out to be the best pineapple upside-down cake I'd ever tasted. The cake's texture was unique: kind of firm but light at the same time. I tried to re-create the effect of Italian durum wheat flour by adding a little whole-wheat flour to the batter. It is not especially sweet, so I serve it with sweetened whipped cream or vanilla ice cream.

Preheat your oven to 350°F. Position a rack in the top third of the oven.

In a large bowl, beat together ¾ cup sugar, the egg yolks, lemon zest, ½ cup of the reserved pineapple juice, the brandy, and vanilla until blended. Sift in the flours, baking soda, and salt; mix until smooth. Stir in the melted butter.

Heat the remaining ½ cup of sugar in a 10-inch cast-iron skillet over medium-high heat until the sugar melts and lightly caramelizes, about 5 minutes, rotating the pan often. Immediately remove the pan from the heat and continue to rotate to cool slightly. (The few remaining sugar crystals will melt in the residual heat while you are rotating the pan, so be careful not to over-brown the

INGREDIENTS
¾ cup sugar + ½ cup sugar
3 large eggs, separated
Grated zest of 1 lemon
1 (20-ounce) can sliced pineapple packed in its own juice, drained, juice reserved
2 Tablespoons brandy or dark rum
1 teaspoon vanilla extract
1 ¼ cups unbleached all-purpose flour
¼ cup whole wheat flour
1 ½ teaspoons baking soda
½ teaspoon salt
8 Tablespoons (1 stick) unsalted butter, melted
1 cup chopped pecans or walnuts
Whipped cream or vanilla ice cream, to garnish

sugar while cooking.) Lay enough pineapple slices in the bottom of the skillet to cover (usually 7 or 8 slices), and sprinkle on the chopped nuts.

Beat the egg whites into soft peaks. Mix about a quarter of the whites into the batter; then fold in the remaining whites until blended. Spoon the batter evenly over the pineapple, taking care not to disturb the nuts, and spread with a metal spatula.

Bake in the top third of the oven until the cake is lightly browned on top and the center springs back when gently pressed with a finger, 25 to 27 minutes. Remove the skillet from the oven, run a knife around the inside edges, and carefully invert the cake onto a plate. Cool on a rack, cut into slices, and serve with whipped cream or ice cream.

Chocolate Chunk–Pecan Cookie Sundaes with Salted Caramel Sauce

Serves 12

This dessert is decadence personified: luscious pecan-chocolate chunk cookies topped with great ice cream, and a "to die for" salted caramel sauce. The cookies are baked and served in individual cast-iron skillets. Although the recipe serves 12, bake as many cookies as you have guests and pans, and keep the remaining cookie dough and sauce in the refrigerator in covered containers. Or, freeze individual balls of dough and bake them whenever you want a special dessert. To serve 12, you could also bake one large cookie in a 10-inch cast-iron skillet and bring it to the table while still warm.

INGREDIENTS

1 stick (8 Tablespoons) unsalted butter, at room temperature, + butter to grease pans

½ cup firmly packed dark brown sugar

½ cup sugar

1 large egg

1 teaspoon pure vanilla extract

1 cup + 2 Tablespoons unbleached all-purpose flour

½ teaspoon baking soda

¼ teaspoon salt

1 cup coarsely chopped dark chocolate chunks (about 6 ounces)

½ cup coarsely chopped pecans

Salted Caramel Sauce (page 96)

Vanilla or chocolate ice cream

Preheat your oven to 350°F. Grease as many 6-inch cast-iron skillets as you will use or a 10-inch skillet with butter.

In a large bowl, cream the butter and sugars until smooth.

Stir in the egg and vanilla. In another bowl, combine the flour, baking soda, and salt. Add the dry ingredients to the butter mixture and stir until smooth. Mix in the chocolate chunks and the pecans.

For each cookie, scoop out a level ¼-cup measure of the dough (or weigh out 2-ounce portions on a kitchen scale) and put the dough in the center of the 6-inch pan.

Repeat until all the pans are filled, then put them in the oven and bake until the cookies are lightly browned, about 13 to 15 minutes. Remove the pans and let them cool until the cookies are warm, not hot. (Alternatively, put the dough into the 10-inch skillet, flatten into a 1-inch thick disc, and bake at 325°F until done.)

Place a scoop of ice cream on each cookie (or cut the large cookie into 8 to 12 slices while still warm), drizzle on the caramel sauce, and serve.

Aunt Ellen's
Delicious Kitchen-Tested Dishes

❈ ❈
CONFECTION WAFFLES

For tender, delicate Confection Waffles, use one cupful of rice boiled to a mush, and rubbed through a sieve; add two well-beaten egg yolks, two tablespoonfuls of sugar, one-half teaspoonful of salt—and beat until velvety. Measure out one cupful of flour sifted once with two teaspoonfuls of baking powder, and measure out a cup and a half of rich milk and melt one tablespoonful of butter. Add the flour and the milk alternately to the egg and rice mixture, beating hard; whip in half a cupful of finely chopped nut meats; then fold in the stiffly beaten whites of the two eggs, and the melted butter. Cook on hot Waffle Baker, and serve with hard sauce.

❈ ❈

❈ ❈
FRENCH MELANGE

Ever eat a bouquet of flowers? French Melange is like that, really! Use two cupfuls of chopped rhubarb (tender stalks that have been put through the coarse blade or your Food Chopper without peeling them). Use two cupfuls of pineapple also chopped, and one cupful of fresh strawberries cut in quarters. Cover with four cupfuls of granulated sugar and let stand for an hour. Then put over the fire in the clean dry Skillet, stir once or twice; cover the Skillet, and let cook slowly over low heat for half an hour. By this time the Melange should begin to thicken. Add a half cupful of shredded almonds or walnuts and tablespoonful of grated orange rind. Leave uncovered and let cook till thick and clear. Stir very little during entire cooking process—distinct bits of fruit should show all through. Pour into glasses dipped in hot water and let cool before covering with paraffin. Serve on nut-buttered bread at tea.

❈ ❈

Chocolate Omelet Soufflé
Serves 4

If you are a chocoholic who loves simple yet intensely rich indulgences, Joe DiMaggio's dessert is a real treat and easy to make.

INGREDIENTS

¼ cup coarsely chopped walnut pieces

1 teaspoon vanilla

8 ounces semisweet chocolate, melted

4 large eggs

⅓ cup heavy cream

3 Tablespoons clarified butter

3 Tablespoons confectioners' sugar

Sweetened whipped cream, to garnish

Preheat your oven to 425°F. Toss the walnuts with the vanilla. Scatter them on a baking sheet lined with aluminum foil and bake in the oven for 5 to 6 minutes, watching that they don't burn.

In a bowl, beat the eggs and cream to blend; add the melted chocolate and beat vigorously until frothy.

Heat a 10-inch cast iron skillet over medium heat until just hot, about 3 minutes; add the butter and walnuts, and cook for 30 seconds. Pour in the egg-chocolate mixture and cook for 1 minute. Transfer the skillet to the oven and bake until slightly firm, 8 to 9 minutes. Remove from the oven, and immediately invert the omelet onto a 10-inch plate. Dust with confectioners' sugar and cut in wedges, serving each portion with a generous dollop of whipped cream.

SAUCES & STOCKS

Red Pepper–Yogurt Sauce
Serves 6

In the jar of an electric blender or food processor, purée the bell pepper, garlic, and salt with the yogurt until smooth. Scrape into a small bowl and stir in the olive oil. Add the mint just before serving.

INGREDIENTS

1 large roasted red bell pepper (from a jar is fine), blotted dry

1 clove garlic, peeled

¼ teaspoon salt

2 Tablespoons Greek-style (thick) plain yogurt

1 Tablespoon extra-virgin olive oil

2 Tablespoons chopped fresh mint leaves

Cucumber-Yogurt-Mint Sauce
Serves 4

In a small bowl, combine the cucumber, yogurt, and salt and pepper to taste. Add the mint. Use this on the stuffed peppers if desired.

INGREDIENTS

1 small cucumber, peeled, seeded, and finely diced

1 cup thick Middle Eastern–style plain yogurt

Salt and freshly ground black pepper

Chopped mint leaves, to garnish

Salted Caramel Sauce
Makes about 2 cups

INGREDIENTS

1 ¼ cups sugar

⅓ cup water

3 Tablespoons light corn syrup

1 cup heavy cream

5 Tablespoons unsalted butter, at room temperature

1 ½ teaspoons coarse sea salt, finely crushe

In a medium saucepan, combine the sugar, water, and corn syrup and bring to a boil over high heat. Cook until the syrup turns a rich amber color, about 6 minutes, swirling the pan and washing down any crystals on the sides of the pan with a wet pastry brush to prevent them from burning. Remove the pan from the heat and whisk in the cream (it will bubble up, so be careful), butter, and salt. Set the sauce aside and serve warm.

Vegetable Stock
Makes about 2 quarts

One of the easiest ways to collect fixings for vegetable stock is to get in the habit of keeping vegetable trimmings including onion skins; carrot, turnip and potato peelings; and those wonderful dark green tops of leeks and celery hearts. Lots of chefs use papery onion skins in their stocks since they add color. The trick is to keep all the fixings in good condition. Unless you gather them within a day or two, it's best to freeze them in a resealable plastic bag, with all the air squeezed out, until you have a sizeable quantity. My vegetable stock differs each time I make it. What follows is a general plan. Don't forget lots of onions and garlic.

INGREDIENTS

1 Tablespoon canola or other vegetable oil

5 large carrots, peeled and coarsely chopped

3 large unpeeled yellow onions, coarsely chopped

3 large stalks celery including leaves, coarsely chopped

2 large leeks, trimmed, rinsed, and split in half lengthwise

2 large cloves garlic, split

Leftover bell peppers, turnips, tomatoes, etc., chopped

2 quarts water

½ cup warm water

4 large sprigs flat-leaf parsley

3 sprigs fresh thyme

1 bay leaf

Salt and black pepper

Preheat your oven to 375°F. Brush a large, flat roasting pan with a little oil.

Scatter the chopped vegetables in the pan, turning to coat them evenly, and roast until they are a rich dark golden brown, turning often, 40 to 55 minutes depending on the size. Be sure they don't burn. Remove the pan from the oven and transfer the vegetables to a deep pot. Add the 2 quarts of water, parsley, thyme, and bay leaf, and bring to a boil.

Meanwhile, stir the warm water into the roasting pan, scraping up the browned cooking bits with a wooden spoon, and add it to the pot. Cover and simmer until the vegetables are very soft, 1 to 1 ½ hours, and then strain through cheesecloth into a clean pot. Season to taste with salt and pepper. Cool and refrigerate until needed. It will keep for 3 to 4 days in the refrigerator. Or freeze for up to 3 months in airtight containers.

"The Secret of Good Cooking is: First, be a critical judge—know excellent cooking from poor cooking; Second, find a fascination in the science, and become thoroughly familiar with 'what, and what not to do'; Third, find a genuine pleasure in the practice—mastering the basic recipes and the operation and control of your Range—and above all, 'THINK.'"

—Aunt Ellen

APPENDIX

Cast-Iron FAQs

By David G. Smith

What does it mean to season a pan?

Seasoning is the process used to protect bare cast iron from rusting, provide a non-stick surface for cooking, and prevent food from interacting with the iron of the pan. The process oxidizes the iron to form magnetite, the black oxide of iron (as opposed to rust, the red oxide of iron). Seasoning is a three-step process: First, the cookware needs to be cleaned well to expose the bare metal (using oven cleaner or lye), applying a layer of vegetable fat, and heating the cookware to bond the fat to the metal. Using the cookware continues to season it as foods deposit oils or fats on the pan.

What happens to the fat? Can it get rancid?

When the fats (vegetable shortenings work best) are placed in the hot pan, it saturates the pan's surface. The heat after repeated uses gradually turns the fats to carbon creating the non stick surface—that's why seasoned pans are black. You need to make sure to wipe out the pan well, until it holds only a dull sheen. If you leave any melted fat on the pan, it can turn rancid over a period of time.

Why can't I use detergent on my pan?

Chemicals in detergents are designed to break down oils, so detergents will break down the very fats you want working for you.

What if my pan is "pre-seasoned"?

A pre-seasoned pan is sprayed with oil after it's manufactured, and baked at high temperatures to achieve iron oxidation. The oil seeps into the pores of the metal and the pan is ready to be used, although it's recommended that it should be re-seasoned. A pre-seasoned skillet is black, while an unseasoned skillet is silvery gray.

Could my pan be coated with wax?

Yes, an unseasoned new pan might be sold with a protective coating (wax or shellac). This coating must be removed (typically by scouring) to expose the bare cast iron surface before the pan is seasoned.

Is it ever "too late" for a cast-iron pan?

Unfortunately, yes. If the pan has a crack in it, or is rusted to the point where the surface is pitted—if the rust has actually eaten holes right through the cast iron—you won't be able to get these back to working condition.

Glossary

AL DENTE usually referring to pasta or vegetables that are cooked until just tender yet retaining some "bite."

BASTE to moisten the surface of foods with a liquid or fat while cooking.

BLANCH to partially cook foods in boiling water to set the color, remove an outside skin (such as with nuts), or to soften the texture of vegetables. In many cases, vegetables are immediately plunged into cold water to stop the cooking and retain the color.

BOIL to cook food in rapidly bubbling liquid.

BRAISE a moist-heat method of cooking foods in a covered pan.

BROIL to cook foods under a direct heat source. (Grilling is the same but the heat source is below the food.)

BROTH/STOCK the liquid derived from slowly simmering, herbs and aromatic root vegetables in large quantities of water. The foundation for many dishes.

CHOP to cut into coarse, irregular pieces.

DEGLAZE to stir a liquid into a hot pan that has been used for sautéing or roasting foods, thereby incorporating and dissolving the browned cooking solids that remain in the pan. A good source for pan sauces and juices.

DICE to cut foods into small, uniform cubes.

GRATINÉ to run food under a broiler to add additional color.

JULIENNE to cut foods into thin, matchstick-like strips.

MINCE to chop finely.

POACH to submerge foods in a gently simmering liquid.

PURÉE to turn a solid food into a semi-liquid state.

REDUCE to boil a liquid to reduce the volume and concentrate flavors.

REFRESH to plunge hot food into cold water to arrest the cooking and set the color or to reconstitute, as with dried herbs.

ROAST a dry-heat method of cooking, usually in an uncovered, shallow pan.

ROUX equal parts by weight of flour and fat cooked together to create a thickening agent. It may be cooked to various stages from white to lightly colored to dark brown, depending on its final use.

SAUTÉ to cook foods quickly in a small amount of fat over high heat.

SIMMER the stage just below boil when bubbles just begin to break the surface.

STEAM to cook foods over rapidly boiling water in a covered pan.

SWEAT to soften vegetables in a minimum amount of fat in a covered pan over low heat.

ZEST (V.) to remove the colored outside layer of citrus fruit; (n.) the colorful outside layer of citrus fruit.

About the Contributors

JOANNA PRUESS is an award-winning author who has written extensively on food for the *New York Times Sunday Magazine*, the *Washington Post, Food Arts, Saveur, Food & Wine,* and the Associated Press syndicate. Her most recent cookbooks include *Mod Mex* and *Seduced by Bacon.*

Pruess is well-known in the specialty food business as a consultant, as well as a regular contributor to NASFT's *Specialty Food Magazine* and as a speaker at many shows. She has developed recipes for numerous clients including Bella Cucina Artful Food, Bigelow Tea, Stonewall Kitchen, Sarabeth's Kitchen, More Than Gourmet, Dufour Pastry Kitchens, and Vanns Spices. She founded and was the first director of the Cookingstudio, a cooking school within Kings Super Market in New Jersey, where she had more than 15,000 students in five years.

She and her husband, restaurant critic Bob Lape, reside in the Bronx, New York.

DAVID G. SMITH is a cofounder of the Wagner and Griswold Society, and coauthored *The Book of Griswold & Wagner* and *The Book of Wagner & Griswold*. He was a contributing author to the authoritative kitchenware book, *300 Years of Kitchen Collectibles*, and has had articles published in various antique trade publications. Smith, a judge in upstate New York, has collected cast iron for more than 30 years.

THE GRISWOLD MANUFACTURING COMPANY and THE WAGNER MANUFACTURING COMPANY, which were combined under the leadership of the Wagner brothers in the 1880s, first developed cast-iron, aluminum, and blended-metal cookware. These manufacturers remain a testimony to over a century of dedication to quality and value.

METRIC AND IMPERIAL CONVERSIONS

(These conversions are rounded for convenience)

Ingredient	Cups/Tablespoons/ Teaspoons	Ounces	Grams/Milliliters
Butter	1 cup=16 tablespoons= 2 sticks	8 ounces	230 grams
Cream cheese	1 tablespoon	0.5 ounce	14.5 grams
Cheese, shredded	1 cup	4 ounces	110 grams
Cornstarch	1 tablespoon	0.3 ounce	8 grams
Flour, all-purpose	1 cup/1 tablespoon	4.5 ounces/0.3 ounce	125 grams/8 grams
Flour, whole wheat	1 cup	4 ounces	120 grams
Fruit, dried	1 cup	4 ounces	120 grams
Fruits or veggies, chopped	1 cup	5 to 7 ounces	145 to 200 grams
Fruits or veggies, puréed	1 cup	8.5 ounces	245 grams
Honey, maple syrup, or corn syrup	1 tablespoon	.75 ounce	20 grams
Liquids: cream, milk, water, or juice	1 cup	8 fluid ounces	240 milliliters
Oats	1 cup	5.5 ounces	150 grams
Salt	1 teaspoon	0.2 ounces	6 grams
Spices: cinnamon, cloves, ginger, or nutmeg (ground)	1 teaspoon	0.2 ounce	5 milliliters
Sugar, brown, firmly packed	1 cup	7 ounces	200 grams
Sugar, white	1 cup/1 tablespoon	7 ounces/0.5 ounce	200 grams/12.5 grams
Vanilla extract	1 teaspoon	0.2 ounce	4 grams

OVEN TEMPERATURES

Fahrenheit	Celcius	Gas Mark
225°	110°	¼
250°	120°	½
275°	140°	1
300°	150°	2
325°	160°	3
350°	180°	4
375°	190°	5
400°	200°	6
425°	220°	7
450°	230°	8